FACE TO FACE

THROUGH THE GLASS DARKLY

MY SOUL'S JOURNEY

By Brenda Havlicek

<u>Dedication</u>

I would like to dedicate this work to my dear friend Pastor Kay Broadnax, who has been a pillar of love and support throughout this entire journey. She has traveled down paths of the unknown with me, daring to search out deep things of the spirit realm. We have walked through the fire, we have been illuminated, transformed, and have been enriched with a deeper understanding and knowledge of the metaphysical world. Although we have known each other for approximately 30 years, it was times like these that our souls connected for a higher purpose. "As iron sharpens iron, so one person sharpeneth another (Prov 27:17)."

Table Of Contents

Acknowledgements

First and foremost, I want to acknowledge my husband Richard Sr.

Richard Sr

My love, I thank you for your undying love and support of everything that I put my hand to. You have allowed me the space to grow spiritually and as an individual, the grace to express myself and experience the world and to allow my Goddess to arise. You laid your ego aside just so I can be free, never feeling or acting threatened in any way. In our 37 years, we have come a long way baby! Through trials, temptations, ups and downs, we are still together, stronger and better than ever. We have matured together throughout this experience of a lifetime. You have always seen the best in me and I love you for that! Together, we have learned to appreciate and embrace all the lessons that have come our way. You are a real man, the best man for me. I thank God that it did not break us, but it made us into the people we are today. I could be with you and love you for a thousand years, living our life like its golden!

Melissa Newton

My girl, who would always call me unexpectedly and started our conversation with "Good Morning Beautiful!" Your calls would come during times when it was hard for me to push forward with this book. Your calls meant so much to me. More than you know, and I thank you for that.

Davita Davis

Who helped me from ground zero to understand the realm of the metaphysical. You were a guiding light for me during a time when I could not find my way. I'll never forget how you were a bridge that carried me across deep waters. I just want to say thank you my angel!

My son, Richard Jr.

Thank you for listening to mom, and for believing and trusting in the things that you have helped me to bring together for this book. I appreciate the diligence and time that you have invested in making this book possible. I love how you are not easily swayed by the crowds or follow the leader type. You are always thinking out loud, literally, and living life by your own terms, no matter what. Keep up the good work on your books and projects. I know you're going to make it rain one day soon! Lol!

My son, James

My son James, who has helped me to see the light on so many things, always having a different view of the world. You have caused me to think out of the box. You keep me laughing, making life better!

Janet Myers

To my best friend Janet Myers thank you for your support, love and encouragement in everything that I do throughout my life. Thank you for helping me with the editing of this book.

To my mother and my siblings who have supported me in every endeavor, I have nothing but love for you all! #FamilyGameIsStrong

Introduction

One day I was just pondering the many reasons I should write the rest of my story. I wondered if I could even go through all of this again, unlike my first book in which I had been journaling for many years jotting down notes of events that happened to me. When I finally decided to begin writing again by divine inspiration, it was a struggle because I literally would have to write the story purely from memory. I would sit down at my computer for days on top of days, from months to years, just remembering all that I had been through and going through the different encounters and stages. These events have taken place over a long period of time, approximately a total of ten years, just to get where I am now.

There were a lot of things I had to consider before I would finish writing and releasing this book. Things you will soon discover in the pages of my life story. I truly bare my heart and soul out naked but not ashamed for all to read. Through every wrong and right action or step I have made along this road, it made me who I am today. I can say, "I'm stronger wiser and better."

To that certain individual, you have been the key to unlocking a life changing experience. I'm thankful for you coming into my life.

There are many things about my life, my purpose and being here that was like a puzzling reflection in a mirror. All that I knew was impart and incomplete. Now I see in perfect clarity and know myself as god knows me.

Chapter 1 - The Beginning

In 2010 I published my first book, "It Started at The Church." It was a type of therapy for me, although I had been writing for a long time. It was basically entries from my diary over the course of many, many years. I never thought I would put my personal business out like that, but when life happened to me, whew!

All I can tell you is that it all came pouring out of my soul like a river. The good, bad, and the REALLY ugly from your girl was out for the world to read. My inner spirit said, "Just let it all out of you!" This was a big deal to me because I was the quiet type. I would always keep everything to myself. I was the type of person who believed in not letting folks know your business. I knew when I made the decision to open up and let my story out, it was going to cause me some embarrassment and hurt feelings, and possible criticism. The list could go on and on.

However, I was determined that I would not let these things stop me. The pain I was experiencing in my heart and soul was overwhelming, to the point that I was literally dying. The pain that I held in all those years was slowly killing me. I thought I had been living life, but I truly was not living my best life because I was holding on to all types of baggage. I had all this baggage and no destination in sight. I was stranded. Some of the secrets that I was holding on to happened during different stages of my life. I locked them away in the far crevasses of my heart and mind, never to be remembered or retrieved again. You know the saying, "I'm going to take this to my grave?" Well, it was not going to be so this time around.

My first book "It Started at The Church," described how I was trapped in love and trouble. Writing my first book was therapeutic and has brought me to a place of no return in various aspects of my life. I am now writing a story about my journey and how my life has been resurrected with renewed purpose. I have been transform, or born again so to speak.

I want to share a passage from "It Started at The Church," in which I combine the beginning of the play, with part of the main theme of the book:

There was this gentleman that I dated over 30 years ago; I saw him at a funeral, and we talked briefly. He told me he still loved me, and for the life of me, I can't get what he said out of my mind! For some strange reason, it seems like it brought back things from my past that happened to me. Now it seems like all these feelings, crazy dreams, and memories are just lingering inside my mind. I can't sleep or think and now it feels like my life is just spiraling out of control!

I knew I wasn't myself, and I felt something was wrong with me. This was more than just running into an old flame. I was having memories of things from my childhood that had transpired, memories of the infamous ex and myself. I did not understand where the memories were coming from, but I knew they were my memories, and deep inside I felt different, like day he looked in my eyes at the funeral. I remember that day so well because I felt something hit me in the gut and I was like ooh! What the, just happened to me!

I told my husband and my closest friend about that day. It was like looking through time or a tunnel. It really took me back. I told them I think something is wrong with me. I just didn't feel the same anymore. They both suggested that I see a doctor or psychiatrist or something. "Oh, so y'all think I'm crazy?" They said no, but if you're having all of these problems, go get some help. You know when people start talking about psychiatrist, it's automatically, and you're a nut case, so I was not trying to hear that.

I had a conversation with one of my sisters and told her what was going on with me. I mentioned to her that I felt like I was living in two worlds at the same time. She suggested that I seek some professional help from a psychologist. Well folks, that was three confirmations about seeking help! My sister referred me to a great therapist that she had worked with in the past. After making my appointment, I was hesitant about going, but I HAD to find out if therapy could help me get back on track.

I struggled to get my story out, crying like a baby, but I did it. I overcame all of the thoughts in my mind fighting me about taking this step. The therapy with the psychologist got me back to where I needed to be mentally, emotionally, and of course spiritually. I was in church regularly, but I was not preaching or teaching anymore. I had resigned at that point from my assistant pastor position. I was still there, listening for any leading of the spirit to help me find my way. I needed to take time to get myself together, and minister to myself by whatever means necessary. I continued going to therapy for almost two years. My therapist mentioned to me upon several of our sessions that I had done a lot of work on myself. Most people don't do the work on themselves like you have. That was so good to hear! I knew then that I was on the right path for sure. I was truly trying to get to the bottom of my problem and get back to my life. This was no joke and definitely not a game. After all, ain't nobody got time for that, plus it was costing me a lot of time and money.

Long story short, I got the help I needed. Over a period of time with the therapist, I was able to feel like I no longer was living in two worlds. I finally began to pull my life back together. Therapy helped me understand a lot about my life, from childhood through adulthood, and the impact different relationships had on my mind and self-image.

I got my life back on track! I was ministering again after taking a short hiatus. I moved to another state, back east for several years. I was alone for most of my days and was able to focus on praying and meditating, which helped me pull it all together and ascend above everything I had gone through. I began to live on another frequency and I began to write a monthly newsletter called "Life Highly Flavored" that became a blessing to myself and others. Life was highly flavored because I began to see so much more that was buried on the inside of me that was colorful and full of flavor. I liked what I was seeing in myself, and I wanted to live my life with color and flavor from that day forward.

I was not preaching or teaching at this time. I would on occasion, only if someone asked me to speak at their event. My new platform was speaking with my ink pen and computer on the printed page. Next up, over a short period of time, I started my *Life Highly Flavored conferences.* During this time, I stopped writing and speaking at the conferences because I began to go through another period of discovery. I started to wonder to myself, when is this ever going to end? I still had questions that no one was able to answer for me. This was partly because of a specific thing I needed an answer for, and I was keeping it to myself. I needed help getting back into one piece in my mind and back to living in one world. The thing that I was keeping to myself was about the other world I was experiencing. I knew that I needed a different type of therapist than the one I worked with before. The questions that I had in my mind were wild and I didn't want anyone to think I was losing my mind or that I was having some sort of psychotic episode that needed medication. We all know that folks will do that!

That was not about to happen to me. One thing I did not allow throughout my therapy was to take any medications whatsoever. Let me be clear, I am a firm believer that there is nothing wrong with taking medicine if needed. If a person has to take a little to help them navigate through their issues, there is nothing wrong with that. However, it just wasn't for me. I do not take any medications on a regular basis at all. Anyway, I just moved forward in my life and decided I would seek out the help I needed. I knew the spirit would guide me where I needed to go, and he would allow me to get the answers I needed in its time. Amen to that!

Going through this traumatic situation, I had to come face to face with some very deep revelations about my life. I was finally in a good place and began to move forward when out of nowhere, that relationship from the past came through like damn wrecking ball! Word to Miley. I was having waking dreams and memories of stuff I didn't experience in this life. The feelings that I had for him were seeping through just like it did in the beginning of the run-in meeting. I did not understand it. Where was all of this coming from? I did not remember doing this stuff with the ex. The places and things that were in my dreams looked like they were from different eras. We looked different at times, but I knew it was him and me interacting in the dreams. It was like having a déjà vu moment. Y'all know what that feels like! If you have never experienced one, it's like I have been here before, I've done that before, and I feel like I know this person, but I have never met them until now.

DEAR GOD, IF YOU ARE LISTENING, CAN YOU HELP A SISTER OUT!? HELP ME UNDERSTAND WHAT IS HAPPENING.

Chapter 2 - The Discovery

I mentioned in the very beginning of my story that I had a very traumatic experience when coming into contact with the ex. I don't know why it happened, but it did. That day we ran into each other at the funeral, he just happened to come outside to the church parking lot at the same time I was on my way to get my car. He began talking to me about the death of his loved ones. I kept it brief and said a few words of comfort back to him. He interrupted and said, "Stop talking," and looked into my eyes. As he stared into my eyes, I stared back into his and I felt something hit me in the pit of my stomach. I was like OH! I have to go! I felt like I was moving through a tunnel or some sort of time warp. From that day until now, it triggered something inside of me. The feelings and memories from my childhood, dreams, etc., began coming fast and furious over a period of time. This was not a game I was playing, let me tell you! It has taken a lot of years to bring myself and all of this to a place of understanding and wholeness. In time, I really began to realize and understand I was experiencing something more than buried feelings and memories. This happened to me in the moment, in the twinkling of an eye. Everything I believed thought I knew, and how I lived my life changed. My life started to unfold like a scroll and from that moment until now, its been like watching a movie about myself!

I'll begin with the very first memory that was puzzling to me. This memory caused me to grieve again as if I had lost someone or if someone had died. That feeling was dealt with accordingly during therapy and I was able to move forward. The first memory I had was of a lady walking in a field and crossing over into a mass of water while crying. She was crying uncontrollably. She was leaning over with this child, whose eyes were filled with terror. I did not recognize her at first, but somehow I knew it was me. I looked different. I was dressed different, not in modern day clothing as I would today. I had absolutely no doubt it was me. I was experiencing grief and pain in my body during the dream of losing this person. I was able to see the person; it was a male child. He was lying there lifeless and I could see he was dying. It felt like my stomach and soul was about to fall out of me. I was dying on the inside, along with him, as he was looking at me with terror in his eyes. I woke up crying and grieving like someone had died for real. It was just a dream I told myself. Or was it?

I thought to myself, I recognize those eyes. They were filled with pain but simultaneously beautiful. They were the same eyes I saw at the funeral that caused me to feel like I was trapped in a time warp. The pain that I felt in my stomach, it was us! Oh my god, it was us, from a different lifetime. I believe that feeling of grief had transcended into my waking life and now I recognized the feeling I was having that led me to seek therapy. It was like I was carrying a baby in my womb. I was so connected with this feeling; it is truly unexplainable. I couldn't get his eyes out of my mind, even while I was awake. I felt like I was there in the dream. I questioned was it really a dream? Those eyes just melted my whole being.

I dealt with this for a while, wondering if I was tripping but stopped when I experienced the same thing over and over again. I knew this was real! I cried about what was happening and I felt a mixture of emotions that I have never felt before in my life, and I didn't know how to deal with what was happening.

I was like no, not this time. I'm not going to see any therapist about this, the devil is a lie! This is all a dream (in my Biggie voice). I had to get hold of myself. It took every ounce of strength I had to pull myself together. During my prayer and meditation time, I heard the spirit speak to me and tell me that "this is not just a dream. I've allowed you to be catapulted into that dimension so you will begin to ask yourself, and me, the questions you have been praying about and for interpretation of this dream. I have come to bring you understanding and to reveal to you at this appointed time what this dream and the memories are all about." The spirit of the Most High God said this is your season to be awakened out of your sleep. Whoop, there it is!

Now, there is something I must tell you about myself for those of you who do not know me. I'm not some "fly by night" who just woke up and began talking about the spirit said this, and the spirit said that. I'm not trying to give you a "I Had a Dream" speech. Let me be clear hunty, Mrs. B comes with the receipts about my spiritual walk in life. Like Lady Gaga said, "I was born this way," okurrr! I can remember back to when I was four years old. I used to tell people stuff before it happened or have dreams and visions that would be on point. When I was a child, I remember asking my mother how does it feel to die? Does it hurt? How did I get back here? Of course, she was baffled, asking me why am I asking her that. There were a lot of things that I said to my parents that made them ask, what the hell is wrong with this lil' baby? I recall when my grandma was told of a specific thing, I told my mother. She said to my parents that there is nothing wrong with her, she just has a gift. As a child, I was like nobody has given me anything, hmm! Believe me; I'm not here for the drama or the smoke. I'm not perfect; I've made some wrong choices in life but have never been caught up in some trash. I think it's very important that I put this in the book. Anyway, let me get back to the rest of my story.

This was just an insight to a part of my life regarding my visions and dreams. Having something like this coming straight out of the blue was crazy! Although I had dreams and visions of past and present events that would come to pass, I have never experienced anything like this. This was something that was on an entirely different level. I believed what I saw in the dreams and made a conscious decision to see where this would lead me. What should be my first step trying to figure out how? What should I do with all that I have uncovered?

Chapter 3 - The Awakening

I found myself between a rock and a hard place. Should I not try to find out what was really happening to me? I prayed about it, talked to a few friends, but of course no one wanted to hear about this relationship anymore. Only one of my friends hung in there with me. She didn't think I was off or nuts at all. She said "Girl, things happen in this life that we can't always explain, but God allows us to experience and learn things as forerunners in truth." God knows, I'm not afraid to tell the truth or worry about what folks may think.

I know it probably looked and sounded like I was hung up on the ex. Well, yeah, maybe to a point. All of this stuff was very real, and the feelings were very fresh like a loaf of baked bread blowing in the wind. Emotions were all over the place. I prayed about how to move forward for a very long time. It was not a rash decision. Finally, the spirit had spoken to me and said, "I'm going to take you on a journey." I knew right from the get-go that this was going to be the ride of a lifetime. I felt like John the Revelator on the isle of Patmos in the Book of Revelations, when the spirit spoke, and he heard the voice he had to follow. Only this revelation wasn't about me! My truth, my purpose, I knew I was going to have to walk it out. I could not be afraid of the process and where it would lead me. I knew that one day I would eventually have to write about this experience. This was not the everyday norm that you hear about. It has been a long, long time coming. Though it is very fulfilling, it is bittersweet at the same time.

I was awakened by the spirit to this truth. The truth is that I discovered that I have lived before this lifetime. I believe I have been here many times; however, I don't have memories of each lifetime. I do believe that the memories that have resurfaced are from my last transition before the life I am living now. For whatever reason, this happened to me. I needed to finish my course, a life lesson that I can't tell why just yet. All I can tell you at this point is what I've experienced to the best of my ability. After piecing things together here and there, the past life memories, relationships, and the now, I was able to find a starting point on my very first encounter. I remember something I had written in my journal back when I was writing about the relationship with my ex and what we shared. Basically, it's a word that just came to me in which I had no knowledge of. My family and friends would always use the term "old flame" for boyfriends or guys/girls that we really liked. So, I said we were kind of twin flames. I started wondering why I wrote that. Twenty plus years later, I find myself looking that word up to see if it even existed and Whala! Bam! There it was!

I began to read up on this. It was so me and what I was feeling inside while simultaneously happening to me. You could put our picture next to the definition! Really, I didn't know what to do about everything that I had read, but it felt so right. I kind of threw it out there in conversation one day when I was talking to my good friend. We had many discussions, and she knew everything from day one about what I have been going through, even before I was awakened to all of this information. We prayed about it and asked the spirit for guidance and direction from the universe. Something came to me so clear one day, and I felt lead to read the bible about Adam and Eve. I'm just going to stop right here! I'm just asking you to stay with me because you are about to go on a journey, so buckle up!

"So, the Lord God caused a deep sleep to fall upon the man, and he slept; then he took one of his ribs and closed up its place with flesh. And the rib that the Lord God had taken from the man he made into a woman and brought her to the man." Genesis 2: 21-22.

Now, let me explain this on how it was given to me. You know how people say, "cut from the same cloth"? Y'all the same to people! The same as a twin flame. Twin flames are a soul connection but not the same as soul mates. It is like the Yin and the Yang, masculine and feminine energy together. Before we come into this flesh at different times, we were together in spirit form. We were split from one another throughout transitions and lifetimes. Transition is the process or period of changing from one state or condition to another. Lifetimes are the duration of a person's life. Transitions are periods of lifetimes that you may have been together; it could be hundreds or thousands of years. I don't know the determining factors of how time works in this. Many years may have passed that you end up back in time together to work out karma, life lessons, or healings before returning back into oneness like you were in the beginning.

I've heard that some twin flames have come together and live their life in this current lifetime, but that is few and far in between. For those who have matured enough and worked through the karma and lessons that is a guarantee that they will come together and balance the energy of divine masculine and feminine in order to be one. They are the ones who light the way for all of us who are searching for answers and truth. It may not be your season to go through or be awakened to this but there are many people like myself who are experiencing this in this life. This situation will definitely get you to thinking or awakening to new thoughts or concepts of living. The purpose is to understand and adapt to new things as we are changing in society to accept many ideals and understand how to accept people for whom and what they are without all the dogma. We say we love, but do we really love when it comes to accepting things out of the norm? Have we truly learned to love unconditionally even when it goes against your belief system?

When I first started going through this there was hardly any talk about this twin flame stuff. Now, more people have awakened to this fact and are running around looking for their twin flames because of the chatter or they hear about this experience like it's cute and fun. Please! You don't go looking for this, it just happens by divine awakening and fate. It is fate that brings this experience your way. No one in their right mind would just start going through this with all the highs and lows that are involved in this type of relationship. This stuff will make you cry and literally drive you right out of your mind. Like I said in the beginning, I was born again but my outlook on everything has been renewed.

I was excited while learning about all of this. I knew that if we (my ex) talked again, I would share some of this and just ask him again if he felt like it was something different about the connection we had. He is a deeply spiritual person, a dreamer like myself, so I knew he would definitely listen to me without thinking I'm tripping. We lived in different cities but had some telephone conversations and I couldn't wait until the next time we would talk.

Years later I was driving to lunch, my friend was in the car with me and she was on the phone talking with someone about Akashic records, and Akashic therapy. I had never heard the word Akashic before in my life and I couldn't wait for my friend to get off the phone so I could hear about her conversation. She had been talking to a young lady that we both knew who was into the metaphysical and had great understanding and education in this field. She was one of the people who helped me get a grasp on my life when it spun out of control. I really didn't know much about metaphysical teachings, just surface stuff. I was not involved in the metaphysical studies other than meditation. I was being nosy, listening in on some stuff being said and I wanted to ask a few questions because it seemed like it could be instrumental in helping me.

After my friend ended her phone call, she made another call, this time to the Akashic therapist. The therapist explained the purpose of Akashic therapy and how it could help me. Once I understood what it was and how it could help me, I made an appointment. Right off the bat, my spirit was jumping for joy! I knew it was what I needed and didn't waste any time because my spirit was telling me it's what I had asked from the universe.

I went to the therapy session by myself. It was awesome, it wasn't weird or anything. The therapy is called Past Life Regression/Akashic Records. Past life regression is a therapy that uses hypnosis to recover what practitioners believe are memories of past lives or incarnations. Akashic records are a compendium of all human events, thoughts, words, emotions, and intent ever to have occurred in the past, present, or future. They are believed by theosophists to be encoded in a non-physical plane of existence known as the Etheric plane. This is really about the origin of you! I did not have to tell them anything or divulge anything other than I was experiencing lots of visions and dreams. The information I needed just came forward during the session. MY GOD! Everything I was experiencing, feeling, and dreaming about was confirmed and I felt like this gave me some validation from someone other than me. I felt strengthened and enlightened. I felt so free; it was like a tingling that I felt all over me.

This was just the beginning; this was the door I needed to open in my life. The main things that opened for me that day had nothing to do with what the therapist said or did. They were only things between me and my creator that he allowed me to remember. Certain things He said and showed to me during my childhood. I had no doubts of what was being said to from the therapist. I was not going to worry about what anyone else thought or said. I told my friend everything that was said in the therapy session and she said "Gurrrlll!" My God, you know you were right all along!"

After that day, I went home and told my husband everything and he said "Wow, that is awesome. You told me this so long ago and the therapist comes along years later and tells you the same thing!" I thank God for my friend who is very spiritual and highly respected woman. She has been a source of accountability for my protection along with my husband so that I am not out here all Willy Nilly.

I'll share with you a few things my therapist talked to me about in regards to grieving and where it was stemming from. We talked about me transitioning here from other lifetimes. My ex and I were together and I suffered great loss with him. This is why I was grieving, and it started from the day I ran into him. It set off a trigger in me, more than likely it came from the look when we gazed into each other's eyes. We have been together in many lifetimes, each having different roles. I had a little more work to do and this was almost finished. My work with him is about to be complete. We had made many soul contracts to be together and there were still things that needed to be cleared up so I could move forward.

Now, when I look back, I understand as a child why I was always feeling sad. I was a loner but now we would call it depression. I always wondered why I felt like this throughout my life. We came back to finish our work together. I didn't understand what I needed to work on with him. It was not told to me by the therapist or revealed to me by the spirit. She did say that I would see him again and that I would be able to work through this to finish the lessons the spirit set forth for me to do.

She revealed that I have been with my husband and that he is my destined mate. He has been and still is your protector and you can live with him for a thousand years. I cried like a baby, but they were tears of joy, not pain. There were many reasons that I can't even begin to explain to you. I know all of this sounds pretty wild, but I am keeping one hundred percent with you. My husband said to me, "If you think it's something more to discover out here for you and you need to see where it leads you, go for it, I'm behind you. I trust you of course but you're going to have to explain your findings to me so I can understand what is happening with you and how this may affect our life." The journey truly began to take shape after my husband told me to go for it and I did.

I began talking to two of my friends briefly about this journey I was about to embark on. One of my friends just blew off what I was saying about past life and other things. She just let me know point blank that she is not here for this. She was like, "Gurrll, you better get some help; I think your obsessed with him. You're going to end up losing your husband behind this nonsense." I told her that he told me to go search it out and see what the outcome is, so I don't see what the problem is if he with me on this. I'm not mad at what she said because that was definitely a possibility. It was a big risk and I would have to pay a heavy price by taking that kind of chance. My other friend who has been with me the entire length of this journey echoed something similar. She was like, "I don't know about all of this. It's new to me but hey, I'm with you. Let God guide you, if this is what he is allowing you to do in order to get your life on track again."

Let the church say Amen somebody!

Chapter 4 - Face to Face

After discovering my past life twin flame information, it accelerated my spiritual awakening. I had to figure out how I was going to make sense of all of this in my day to day life and why this was so important for me to know. Why now? After previously living without all of this knowledge, what difference was it going to make now that we have both moved on with our lives? I am now wide awake, and I can't just lay here without finding out everything I need to know. How was I going to do that without opening up some old doors, wounds and feelings? Damn Gina! Yep, I had to really walk it out. I had to take it one day at a time, step by step in hopes that it would bring more clarity to my path and the end result. The first thing I wanted to do was to have a conversation with the ex about what I had discovered. I wanted to ask him more questions about myself and if he had been experiencing some of the same things such as past life memories or dreams of me. I wanted to talk to him about our old relationship again as there were some things we talked about back then that I felt would help me. I wanted to ask him if he still remembered the times we had conversations about how we both felt we had known each other before.

I know, DON'T DO IT GURL! DON'T OPEN THAT DOOR AGAIN! Well guess what? I opened that door, yes I did that! In doing so, I opened up a whole can of whoop ass on myself. A WHOLE CAN. I didn't make a call to talk to him right away. However, life changed for me and I ended up living in the same city as he did. Although we lived in the same city, I never ran into him. We had mutual friends and family in the city and after being there for a while, we ended up at an event in which we both knew we would be in attendance. We just said hello to one another in passing and went about our business. When we finally did run into each other it was just one of those times the universe allows you to cross paths. I was like, "Hey, what a coincidence we ran into each other at the mall of all places." I said, "I am glad we did, because I have been praying I would get a chance to talk to you and I just didn't now how that would happen. I guess us meeting today was meant to be." He said, "Really? Well, what do you want to talk about? I have some time; we can just talk out here." I said, "Okay, cool."

First, he said, "Girl, you still look good." I said, "Thank you, you got that salt and pepper working for you, looks good on you." He said, "Well thank you. You look so young and pretty EVERY TIME I do get to see you. You never age; you're going to look young all the time like your mother." I said, "Thanks, but anyway, I have a few questions I need to ask you." "Ok, shoot," he said. So I asked, "Do you remember when we ran into each other at the funeral back then?" He said, "Yeah." I said, "Well, since then I ain't been the same. The question I have is have you ever had this feeling or connection with anyone else like the one we have?" He shook his head and said, "No." I was like really? "Well, I think we have been together before, like in a past life. Do you believe in that?" I asked. "Girl, what in the world are you into? Hell nah, to the nah, nah, nah. What's up with you? Something going on?" he asked. I asked him, "Do you remember when we were together, we both said it seemed like we knew each other forever?" He looked and said, "Yeah, but what does it matter now that we have moved on with our lives?" "I think we have been here before, together in a past life. I've seen a glimpse of that in my dreams and visions," I told him. He looked and laughed at me, "What!? You on some kind of trip?"

I asked him again, "Okay, so you don't think we have some kind of special connection or bond?" "Well, I didn't say that, but what does it matter now? We have moved on and that was a long time ago" he said. "So, you're saying that you don't have strong feelings for me still or feel this connection even though we have not spoken to each other or seen one another in a long time?" I pleaded. He sat there, looking at me stunned, like a cat had his tongue. I said to him, "I'm not trying to mess up your life or mine, but I'm looking for answers and closure for my life. This just will not go away. Are you over all this now? Because after twenty plus years you were confessing your feelings but now after a couple of years you don't have any?" I questioned him.

"If I'm wrong, tell me so, but I can tell just by talking and looking at you, that I already know the truth," I added. He said, "Well, if you already know the truth, why do I need to say anything?" I looked at him and said, "Because I need you to say it out of your own mouth, your own heart." He paused and just looked at me. He replied, "Yes Brenda, I still feel that connection between us but I'm not experiencing the stuff you are talking about." I said, "Thank you, all I wanted to know is that it's not just me feeling this way." He looked at me and said, "Well, we better get going. We been standing out here for a while now but I'm going to be praying for you." I said, "Thanks for the talk. I appreciate you being open with me." "Anytime you need me you can call me," he said. We laughed and I said, "You know you going to get a spanking if I do call you, because you already know what time it is." He said, "Nah, it's cool, I'm a real grown man. Don't be upset about what I said; just trust God to help you through. Tell your sister I said hello." We both started cracking up. That's a joke between us from back in the day. "It was good to see you again, and you still looking good girl. Take care," He said as we parted ways.

The thing I have come to realize after the door opened for us to have conversation was that it was about me understanding my soul's journey and purpose. However, I knew he would be awakened to this also in God's timing. I knew that day that things were shaken in him and an earthquake was about to happen in him. It was written all over his face. I knew he was ready to get ghost because I was asking him about stuff that was buried inside him and he wasn't trying to go there anymore. I know now that I was too aggressive, and he looked like he was putting on his Forest Gump shoes. Run Forest, run! I know that is one of the dynamics of the relationship of twin flames called the runner and the chaser. I can't blame him if he never wanted to talk or see me again. However, he was running because it was awakening something on the inside of him and it was terrifying. He was having a reaction on the inside that he didn't understand. You can call me the chaser for real because I was in hot pursuit of trying to see anything that was going to get uncovered.

The next time we would talk, he would clam all up like he didn't know who the hell I was or couldn't remember what we talked about on the last conversation. Sometimes, I would act different with him as well. Kind of very matter of factly, even argumentative at times and very defensive, but so was he. We both were like it's my way or the highway. Other times, we were both just very kind and loving towards one another, but it didn't last long before we were back to square one. He got on my last nerves and I got on his as well. We would just say forget you and then would see or talk to each other again, sometimes for a year or two. We were like kids, getting into arguments and not wanting to play anymore, but when we see each other again its one of the happiest times. At first, I did not understand what was really going on. I began to take some mental notes on our back and forth behavior. I began to see certain patterns in both of our behavior. I needed to uncover the real reason behind all of this and if I didn't, everything would all be for nothing.

One reason is because we were both married to other people. I didn't know what to do or expect. Were we going to leave our mates to be together? That would be a no but that's why I had to understand and find out what this connection between us was all about. From the very start, I made it clear I did not want anything from him. I never asked him to leave his wife or get together with me, nor did he ask that of me. I must confess, the thoughts and emotions were a draw. It's always present and it takes two to tango. Neither one of us was willing to go there. If you listen to what other people say about getting back together you can mess your life up. Sometimes it was me and sometimes it was him feeling vulnerable, but we are mature enough to know better. We both very well understood that crossing the line would change things forever in our lives. By starting a relationship again with the twin flame, it would more than likely not work out, especially when you are not enlightened enough to understand the dynamics. There was zero chance of us ever coming together in that way. Sometimes this kind of reminded me of the movie "Two Can Play That Game." It felt like a bunch of mind games, energy always exchanging.

After much examination, I soon discovered a major phase I would go through. Mirror Mirror on the wall. This is the best description for this phase. Just seeing or talking to him allowed me to come face to face with some behaviors in myself that were questionable. Have you ever called somebody out for the same thing you know you're doing as well? It's called spot it, you got it. I mean, I saw the good in him, the bad, and the ugly. I also saw the same thing in myself. This really shook me up and woke me up even more. I slowly felt the scales fall off my eyes. It was like the song says, "I can see clearly now, the rain is gone."

I could see all the obstacles in my way. I noticed times I had conversations with him or seen him, I would have to go through a lot of self-introspection. It was not always a willing thing for me to do but either one or two things were going to happen to me. I was going to have a breakdown from all the stuff that was happening, or I was going to have a breakthrough. I think I had them both at times! I was hurt for multiple reasons I can't begin to tell you about. I did not like some of the behavior patterns I was recognizing in my life. Let me give you one example. It was hard for me to let go of people, places and things. I would hold on for dear life. I noticed for him it was the opposite. He would let stuff go in a heartbeat and not look back. I cared all the time what people thought about me on a regular basis. He could give a damn about what people thought. He always said he would do whatever he felt like doing and not worry about the consequences.

What I need to let you know is how I got over it. Yass baby, I had to go through some deep healing. I'm talking about down to the white meat. Y'all get my drift? There were even times I though I was healed and doing fine, but God let me know with a quickness, I was not finished because something would happen in certain areas I thought I was healed in and BAM! Back to healing waters you go Brenda. I knew when I was healed fo sho when I got drug through the same situation again and there was no pain or feeling. Trust me, you know when you're walking in the victory no matter how many times you get tried you make the grade and graduate to the next level. I had to go through a lot of cleansing a healing. I had to peel back patterns and the layers of the old me and allow the new patterns to arise in my life. It has taken a lot of years to get to this place but I'm here, Hallelujah!

It had been a long time since I had talked to or seen him but once again, we are always in and out of each other's life since the main event first happened. I was out of town and I did not know we would run into each other in another state. I swear this was not something that was planned, that's for sure. Let me explain, we have family in the same state. Our families have known each other forever. I was out eating lunch with a friend and here he comes. I was shocked, wondering what he was doing here in town.   What a surprise! He was there on business while I was visiting with family and friends. I was happy to see him and actually I had told the universe I sure would like to talk to him. I had been telling my other friend for months prior that I feel like something is going on with him. He kept coming to me in my dreams, so I had been praying for him. She said, "You can call and ask his family about him." I was like nah, that's not going to happen. You know how that would look and I'm not going to do it.

We greeted each other and talked for a few minutes. I told him that he had been on my mind so strong a couple of months ago and I prayed for him. He said, "You always know or sense when I'm going through something, don't you?" He thanked me and said, "I have something I'm really going through right now; I could really use some prayer. If you have a moment I can talk to you about it and get your advice." Okay, wow! He must really be going through I thought to myself. I couldn't believe he was being so open about his business. Brother was looking like a black angel that day.   He might have been going through, but you couldn't tell it by the way he was looking. After we finished talking I said, "Got to go brother, but I was so happy to see you." He said, "you're not too happy you aint gave me no hug, handshake, or nothing." I said, "You play too much. Don't start nothing, it won't be nothing." That was just us being silly.

I could tell he had changed a lot. Of course, you know I had to ask him a few things that I had learned about this twin flame process. He didn't have any hang ups like before. He was even interested in talking to me some more about the things I had told him. He was super pleasant; I've never seen him this vulnerable. I felt like he had really evolved and experienced a lot of growth as well. I didn't know if we would see each other or talk ever again, but I got further than I ever did with him and just solidified a lot of things. When I returned from my trip, I was just pondering how we had this by chance meeting and what had taken place. I realized that was paramount to this entire story. Something strange happened to me again that day I was praying for him.

Have you heard of people saying they experienced a déjà vu moment? Well, I had one when he asked me to pray for him and we touched hands in agreement that his prayer would be answered. We both prayed and agreed for his situation and we prayed for blessings on each other's life and family. After the prayer was finished, we said that we would always be friends and if we ever needed each other's help, we would be there for one another. We vowed to be there for each other in the next laugh. We laughed and said yeah right. I realized that is what we have done over and over again in past lifetimes without realizing what we were doing. We just made another soul contract to see each other again. Oh, my Lord!

Sometimes we do and say things into the universe in prayer, not realizing the impact that it may have in our lives. This was paramount for me to be able to understand and recognize how we had been agreeing though God knows how many lifetimes! Man, I'm glad we have come this far just to get to this place of experiencing and evolving as two different individuals in a twin flame union. Whether anyone believes me or not, I know the ex does not comprehend all of this like I do. It has taken many years of trying to understand what has been happening to me from the very first day. I had to allow patience to have its perfect work in my life because you just want this to be done and over with. However, it didn't work like that for me. I was awakened out of a deep sleep. When the spirit woke me up I got up and immediately got out of them grave clothes and began to research and apply all that I had discovered. One thing I was sure of was that I am here for a higher purpose than I ever realized before understanding that I was in a twin flame relationship.

Chapter 5 - Accessing Memories

That Deja vu moment is what I call accessing an old memory from a past lifetime. You know me; I had to put on my detective hat and get to work! I was trying to understand why this always happening to me. It finally hit me! We had been making soul contracts over our lifetimes. Once I realized we just created another soul contract, I was like "no, we're not doing this again!" I immediately broke that contract, because they can be broken.

This was a choice we made that day, not something that was destined. We did not have to create that. I think sometimes we do things out of habit, without having a full understanding of the reasoning behind it. I am researching and studying for a reason. I believe that reason is that I am finishing my course, remembering, clearing, healing, and working out these soul injuries and lessons so that I can make progress in other areas of my life.

I made a choice from the beginning. I didn't close my eyes when I was being showed all of this. I decided to follow the voice and it led me to all of this. I could have ignored it because our choices can intercept the design of destiny. However, I made a destiny decision at that moment not to enter into another contract. I knew I was back in this life because I never made the correct choice in other lifetimes. This was a golden opportunity to ace the test. I was fully aware not of what needed to be done this time around, so let's do this girl!

Something in my brain was continually occurring to me that was out of my control. Something was causing me to access and retrieve these memories. It was like information from the past and present were stored in my brain. I began to research this out to the best of my ability. When déjà vu moments happened, I began to understand something was being stimulated. There was something taking place called recognition. It allowed me to realize that I have seen or done this before, or that it is familiar for me.

Another stage I experienced was called recall. There are three types recall. First, there is Cued Recall. This type facilitates and recovers memories that have been lost. Secondly, there are Free Recalls. With these types you may remember short term or more recent memories of things, but not in order. Last, there are Serial Recalls. These are information or memories are presented in a specific order.

I am not a scientist or Doctor. Nothing even close to that, but I have uncovered enough for me to understand what was going on in my life. This was the spirit taking me on a journey, downloading me with information, and teaching me day by day where to get information. I know there is still so much to learn but I am understanding all that I can. There is so much information that I have studied and uncovered that I would never be able to finish writing this book. I am just giving you some of the steps and processes that have helped to get to the place I am at now.

I also began to realize as my eyes became open that I have been a conduit of connecting others to past life information or people. It is not always a past life male or female relationship or a twin flame situation. Sometimes it has been different. Remember, spirit is not male or female; we are dealing with masculine and feminine energies. So you and I have to deal with the dynamics of experiencing different types of relationships.

People have found children from another life in which they did not understand the connection: the what's, the why's and the how's, but I was able to bring them to understanding in their situation. There have been people who have found each other in other various soul connections. What I can tell you from these connections is that people are so much better off in their life after finding out the truth of their connections. People have come together in marriages through meeting me. It was nothing that they or I planned; it was the universe doing it. There has been so much more information that has come into my life on soul journeys that would probably blow your mind like it did mine in the beginning. One thing that I know is that if God said it, he'll prove it. He will not just tell you, He will show you!

Chapter 6 - Clear as Crystal

It became really clear to me that this relationship was a life lesson for me. It is something that has been a source of deep healing, freedom, purpose, and fulfillment. I have learned so much about myself, the real me. That one encounter has changed my life. There have been some paramount revelations and lessons that I learned from that day until now. That is not to say that I haven't learned lessons from other relationships or people, but this was different. It has been an out of this world experience. I am going to talk about each step that I went on through this journey.

Deep Cleansing

Have you ever taken a shower without soap and also with soap? I had to go through a time of washing my soul, clearing and cleaning out those old hurts, pains and memories. You may not forget them but the pin of all those memories that hold you captive get cleared from removing the pain associated with the memories. You must walk in the new visions of new life and the new experiences that have come into your life that it is not always a past life male/female or twin flame situation your supposed to have. Pain has no power over you unless you hang on to it and do not let go of the old patterns.

Deep Healing

Have you ever wondered why we struggle with certain issues from birth? I believe that it's something in the amniotic water or chemicals in the water bag that washes your memory when transitioning into life or lifetimes while transitioning through the birthing process. I think by design that old cellular memories are to be wiped cleaned, but for some of us, a lot of us have memories that begin to surface throughout life from a previous lifetime because everything did not get totally wiped out by design. I believe it's something in the water because I understand and believe the water that we come through in birth is definitely a portal into this realm from the higher realm of where we come from as a spirit. Once again it's just my thought on all of this, but I'm just sayin'.

At an early age, I began to see certain things about myself and wondered why I had certain behaviors and where they came from. I would ask myself "What is wrong with me?" I was just a kid dealing with the heavy feelings and questions about life. My guess is that I came into this world with these behaviors and thinking patterns already put on me. This is just my theory about what I learned from this experience, but here we go. I believe that some of these issues came into each life with me. No matter how many times I made a transition into this mortal world, apparently I had not finished my work. I did not pass the mark, but this is the season that was appointed to finish and complete the work in this area of my life. My mental and emotional well being has been a challenge I kept going around in circles with. I couldn't break the cycle. I hadn't realized why I kept dealing with the same crap over and over. I learned that you could change places or people, but if you have an issue within yourself, you will continue to have the same problem. The healing and wholeness came as I began to see this face to face and I accept that I had a problem. I needed help and I moved forward in getting that help until the issue was conquered. Once you learn the recipe for healing, you can live in a place of wholeness. If you see things trying to flare up again, just follow the steps in the original healing recipe. Trust and believe that you will be tested again. Believe dat!

Freedom

I experienced freedom in my mind and heart once I recognized, faced, and accepted the truth of my behavior patterns. I learned that the spirit was not trying to change everything about my personality, just the behaviors. They were false imprints of the blueprint of my life that crept in and prohibited me from being the person he created me to be. When I finally began to comprehend where it was, I was getting stuck. My mind began to go on replay for a while before it got it. Whala! It finally stuck. I had to take a snapshot in my mind and keep looking at what was happening to me before I was truly able to turn things around. The freedom did not come all at once, but it was a slow, gradual process. Oh, how blind I was, but the spirit allowed the film to fall off my eyes. When that happened, I was able to see and approach things in a totally different way. I now understand that in order to become free, I had to purge those behaviors and incorporate this knowledge into my life.

Purpose

It has become clear as crystal to me that I walked through a portal of time, sort of like "Back to The Future." I was zapped into this out of world experience, now I'm here in this world again in order to finish my course that had possibly began thousands of years ago. What is the use of living and dying without discovering and understanding your purpose? I have heard people teach or even preach to us about purpose. One thing I found out is that no one can tell you what your purpose is. That is something every individual must discover for themselves. If you do not find out what your purpose is, someone will always try to tell you what they think it is. This will cause you to be forever dissatisfied in life.

To me, purpose is about finding your truth of your reality in this realm and putting on a flesh body to do a specific work. I know I am a spirit being who has lived in many different dimensions and worlds. I have come into this realm to finish a portion of my assignment. Somewhere along the way, our minds have been closed off to where we come from, and who we truly are. I have always been very inquisitive about humanity and the spirit world since childhood. I believe that the spirit allowed me to be enlightened enough when I transitioned into this life, so that I may search out the truth of my existence. Being in the ministry for so many years has given me a door into the realm of the spirit. When I would study the bible, I always wondered why everything was about renewal or replenishment. I always felt like something was missing, like there was some untold truth somewhere. There have been so many gaps in our spiritual learning that people have never talked to us about it, but certain people secretly would like to know. It was my job to fill in those gaps. I can only speak from my experience. Purpose is not some sort of skill you can just do. It is not doing or being the greatest teacher or athlete in the world. That is only a product of your purpose throughout time. We are going to know in part until that which is perfect or complete comes. I do not mean sixty or eighty years from now, but times are seasons. Until we are in complete understanding of our existence, the master will allow us to continue our path until we understand and move into fullness with him.

Fulfillment

There is a peace that has come into my life that I did not have before. I know the peace that surpasses all understanding that guides my heart and mind. That type of peace came into my life as I started to get serious about my journey. I no longer had the time to get involved with what everyone else was doing in their life. As folks would say, "Get you some business and stay out of mine." Not to say I was in people's business, but a lot of the issues I had came from taking on other peoples problems. Believe it or not, that is a behavioral pattern. When I came to that realization, I slowly began to remove that from my life. Unfortunately, that included some people I care about. I didn't have to say a word, I just became unavailable, they just didn't know it. I stopped allowing people to misuse and abuse me emotionally. I had to stop having a victim mentality. I was always keeping my mouth shut to not offend others, thinking they would be like that towards me. I was always putting everyone else's feelings or needs before mine. Ughh, not anymore! I am the same nice, loving individual because that's who I really am. However, if people think they can just use or mistreat me on the sly, then they are sadly mistaken. What I do is just let them think or feel like they have gotten away with it. I just silently move forward and continue cultivating and elevating. I save myself from any heartache by removing my presence. I give it no playground time, because that kind of love and friendship does not live here anymore.

I'm truly fulfilled knowing I'm walking in purpose when I meet people on a similar journey in some of the most awkward times and places. I am fulfilled when I can be a messenger of light and love that can be of guidance to help others on their journey. Now that I have come this far understanding my assignment, I realize that I had to be a forerunner for those coming behind me. For those that might be in the beginning stages on a journey similar to mine. For those that may not understand what to do or where to go, I didn't. There is fulfillment in knowing and learning how to get healing from past life hurts that bleed into my life now. Through much trial and tribulation, I learned to let go of a lot of stuff in the previous life that had become an issue in this one. Sometimes we want to blame people for circumstances that may cause us to behave or respond in a certain way.

I assure you, all the lessons that I have learned were about me and nobody else. That is liberating all by itself! I'm thankful for each and every trial, tribulation, lesson, and healing it has brought into my life. You can't hate the process, you must embrace it. I'm very grateful to the spirit for teaching me how to move forward and cut things out of my life that do not serve me or my purpose, and without hurting others in the process. I can truly say that I no longer live in the things of the past. In this journey, I had to visit things from the past that helped me clear out old energy. However, at one point I kept taking small visits to the same place and almost took up residence there again. I fell into a trap and almost got swallowed up, but God plucked me out and showed me what I was doing. He made a way of escape for me, but I didn't escape the lesson it taught me. This was the hardest lesson I have ever had to learn but I got it! When I closed that particular door and finally seen it for what it was really was, everything just dissipated like magic. Just as quick as the lesson came into my life, it was over. Wow! I can't even believe I went through all of this stuff. It is surreal.

Now everything has been made clear as crystal to me. During the journey through my past life, the twin flame connection has definitely caused me to rise up to a higher place in every aspect of my life. It has brought out the best in me, love and light!

About The Author

Brenda Havlicek is a former ordained Pastor and has worked in various aspects of the ministry in over 30+ years and also is a graduate of Biblical Studies with Honors. She is also the former founder of Life Highly Flavored Conferences, a speaker, a host and author/editor of inspirational new letters. She is the author of her first published book, "It Started At The Church: Trapped in Love And Trouble" and the producer of the stage play, "Trapped in Love And Trouble".

Brenda has been married to her husband for 36 years and they have 2 sons, 1 daughter-in-law, 1 son-in-law, and 5 grandchildren.

Author Brenda Havlicek is back with her new book, "Looking Through The Glass Darkly: Now Face to Face", bringing together and connecting the pages of her previous story from her first book to the final closing of that chapter in this book, yet opening a universe to each of you as you come face to face with new truths.

Her highest hope and purpose is to see others bring forth their story or journey and not be bound by anything or anyone.

SO BE FREE BEAUTIFUL!!

You can connect with me!

On Facebook at Brenda Havlicek

or

Email me at havlicekbrenda@gmail.com.